ROOTS

TO REALITY

BOOK OF POEMS

Catherine D. Netter

Acknowledgements

I would like to acknowledge my two sons, Christian Herbin and Brenton Herbin, who are the driving force in my life. They encourage me each day and always remind me to take time for myself. Presenting this book of poems is my way of doing something for myself and sharing with the world my experiences, perspectives, and realities faced as a black woman, a black mother, and a black descendant of slavery in America.

Introduction

These poetic verses reflect my personal encounters, perceptions, musings, and aspirations all intertwined with an unwavering desire to incite positive change. My words delve into the diverse spectrum of societal occurrences and challenges, spanning from past to present, with an ardent belief that a brighter future is within reach.

The profundity of history's depths is not lost on me. Yet, I remain steadfast in my optimism that we are collectively forging a new path toward a life filled with freedom, equality, justice, and liberty for all. Amidst the turbulence of life, there are moments of sheer elation that come to mind, especially when I think of my beloved sons. It is the love and sagacity of my parents that have nurtured and propelled me forward, inspiring me to hold steadfast to hope and never give up.

Undoubtedly, your vision, like mine, is one where the power of every individual's voice is amplified, and their humanity is cherished and respected. Black Americans have daily concerns that are far-reaching and complex, and we must navigate an array of challenges to protect our mental and physical well-being that others may never have to consider.

The color of my skin is a constant source of scrutiny and

judgment, and we are often subjected to unfair treatment and discrimination. Every time we step outside, we must think about the implications of our presence, from the scrutiny of our appearance in stores to the anguish of witnessing the news cycle's traumatic stories. Our worries extend to the future of our children, and the experiences they will endure as they grow up in a society that is still grappling with the scourge of racism.

The social conditioning, we experience is insidious and far-reaching, with the normalization of negative stereotypes and the normalization of defeat as an acceptable outcome. Our minds also drift to the thoughts of our ancestors, enslaved, and traumatized by a history that continues to be misrepresented and whitewashed in contemporary America.

Even our personal appearance, such as how we choose to wear our hair, can be a source of contention and prejudice in certain environments. The barriers we face in employment are another constant reminder of the pervasive nature of discrimination in our society. In times of turmoil, we seek solace in our faith, yet the question remains whether it is enough to sustain us amidst the trials and tribulations we face daily.

This literary work is not only intended to inform and inspire but also to provoke deeper contemplation and introspection. I acknowledge that the themes of racism, colorism, colonialism, capitalism, slavery, and discrimination can be incredibly weighty and emotionally charged. Living through these experiences is a far greater challenge than merely discussing them.

Therefore, I have included note pages in this book, providing ample space for you to engage in meaningful reflection. As you read each selection, I encourage you to jot down your thoughts, feelings, and interpretations. Use this space to explore your understanding of the underlying causes and roots of our reality, and to consider the ways in which we can work together to bring about a more equitable future. This is a vital step toward fostering empathy, understanding, and progress.

Table of Contents

I Wonder

I sit upon a whipping tree,
wondering one day who I might be.

I wonder when I look ahead,
if I run, will I be dead?

How long will I have to run and hide,
before I make it to the other side?

Is there freedom beyond the sea
or just more pain awaiting me?

That horrible sound of cotton being picked,
bodies dried from the sun and cracked lips licked.

As the countless days grow hard and long,
we try to find comfort by singing a song.

Generations of families working in the field.
How much more time must we yield?

I wonder why
I wonder when
I wonder when my new life can begin

Dark Skin

Lord, why is my skin a darker shade
than my sisters and brothers, you also made?

Is there a reason, I am the color of night
that often forces me out of sight?

When I speak, I am told to be silent
Words of objection are seen as defiant

Prodded, teased, and shoved into submission
I'm expected to move without my own volition

You have the power to move the sun, oceans, and trees
When will you change how others see me?

Wait, what is that I hear you say?
Take your hand and you will guide the way

The color of my skin is not a curse
It sings a song of a different verse

The reason I am met with such a frown
Is that others can see my glowing crown

March on black girl and shine your light
Your stride, your will, can win this fight

Dark skin is magic in all shades and tones
But you must first believe it, right down to your very
bones

Enslavement

We were sitting on the throne
With math and science at our feet
Architects, engineers, queens, and kings
You did meet

Kidnapped, chained, and dragged
To ships in the harbor
Bodies piled on top of one another
Wondering how much farther

Stolen from our homeland
To be unloaded on docks
Pale hands running down our bodies
To be sold on auction blocks

Families separated and made to work
Hundreds of years for free
In this new world filled with hatred
For those who look like me

If I try to escape
Or run away
I will be whipped, tortured, beaten
And forced to stay

That cracking sound of flesh
Being torn from the bone
Not even considered human
Decided by skin tone

Walk with me, Lord
I don't know how much more I can take
The bounds of my soul
Are sure to break

Black Mothers

Another black mother
cries out into the night,
her son has been killed
taken out of sight.

How many more stories
must we read,
before something snaps,
and we can no longer concede?

Lynched, dragged, beaten, or shot,
every day,
a different story,
with the same old plot.

A son pleads and shouts
calling for his mother,
sometimes put to death
at the hands of his own brother.

It's like living in a nightmare
that just won't stop.
Chokeholds, batons, gunshots
that go- POP. POP. POP.

Are we simply expected
just to hold on,
patiently waiting
and checking our phones?

We are living in a constant
state of terror.
Regardless, if we do
or don't make an error.

Black men don't get to live
past perceived mistakes.
When will America,
put on the brakes?

Here comes another sound of sorrow, I hear.
It just keeps on happening, year after year.

Love to Son

I love you, son
More than you will ever know
So much more
Than words can ever show

The day of your birth
Was my greatest joy
"Oh my," I said,
"I just had a boy!"

God is trusting me
With this brand-new life
All the days
Until he takes a wife

Educational events
And little league games
No two days
Were just the same

Reading books
And running in the park
So many days
We stayed out well past dark

Birthday parties
With hugs and kisses
I wanted to extend to you
All your wishes

For as long as I live
I will be cheering you on
Memories created
Long after I'm gone

So, stand tall, proud
And sing your song
My love is with you
All day long

Momma

You sacrificed so much
Every single day
Trying to make sure
Nothing stood in our way

Fried cornbread and collard greens
Was our favorite meal
Eating everything on our plates
That was the deal

Sharing stories and creative arts
Was just a few of your gifts
It was our spirit
You could always uplift

Dedicated to the success
Of your students in class
While making sure in school
We also passed

From kindergarten to college
You pushed us forward
Constantly reminding us
To look onward

Now we are left
With words of appreciation
Thank you, mom
For your deep dedication

A Father's Love

Thank you, dad
For loving me
And showing me all the things
I could not see

That prideful joy
Of a father's love
Has kept me soaring
Far above

When I grow tired
Weary and sad
I think
Of all the memories we had

Speaking events
And getting petitions signed
Listening to political commentary
Was our way to unwind

There was always a reason
To take on a cause
Too much going on
To stop or take a pause

Then one day
Your body gave out
And in all your work
You never sought clout

So, this is my way
Of lifting you up
Systems of injustice
I will continue to interrupt

Pool Game

Has anyone ever explained to you
the billiard game of pool?
Do you know how to play
and understand the rule?

The white ball defeating the black ball
is the ultimate goal,
after all the other balls of color
have been knocked into a hole.

The balls of color
have a number on their back.
Sounds a lot like our prison system
where the majority are black.

If the black ball dies,
before all his homies of color are laid to rest,
the game starts over,
and the balls are reset.

Now many will say,
"Well, it's just a game!"
But hundreds of years later,
and our outcomes are still the same.

In every system and institution
the white ball is on top,
and of all the balls of color,
the black ball is the one we must stop.

Receipt

Do I want a receipt,
did you say?
I'm black in America,
every day.

If I leave this store,
without proof that I paid in my hand,
inside a jail cell,
is where I'll land.

Some think this is crazy,
others think it's too much.
Just shows with our history,
they are out of touch.

Lights, sirens, the police will come
and throw me on the ground.
It won't even matter,
that people are standing around.

Where is the justice,
for people who look like me?
It feels like
we are still being hung from a tree.

And it may not even matter
if I show a receipt.
Chances are,
I will still get beat.

Banning Books

Banning books that tell the truth
About American History
Doesn't guarantee
It will remain a mystery

Regardless,
Where the story unfolds
Facts are being uncovered
And they will be told

Stolen land, kidnapping, and lynching
Just to name a few
Glossing it over with tales of glory
That we know aren't true

The whole idea is not to repeat the same
Acts, laws, and policies, that have brought us so much
shame.
Imagine if we could fully understand
And vow to be a different kind of person, woman, or
man

Talents, intellect, and innovation
Could be unleashed like never before
Cures for illnesses and additional resources
Would be in store

Though,
It seems we would rather lose this race
By holding on to racism
And keeping everyone in their place

Hair Texture

Should the texture of my hair,
prevent me from getting the job?

Do I have to wear my hair straightened,
or cut into a bob?

Typing, writing, and public speaking,
those are the qualifications you say you're seeking.

If I arrive to work with braids, twists, or afro curls,
does that make me less qualified than the other girls?

My character and the quality of my work are all that
should matter.
Instead, it's my hairstyle that's causing all the chatter.

You're sending my intellect, talents, and gifts out the
door.
It makes me wonder, just how many more.

Until we give everyone an equal opportunity,
this will continue to be the struggle of my community.

The Black Church

Attending church on Sunday mornings
Is our way to debrief
Holding hands and gathered in prayer
Trying to find relief

We lay our burdens upon the altar
Trusting everything will be okay
We're taught that God is watching over us
And has promised a better day

That grandma starts rocking
As she belts out a song
Her voice can part the ocean
Make you forget anything is wrong

Hands are waving in the air
Feet are tapping on the ground
The organ starts playing
My, what a joyous sound

The spirit rises too high
For the preacher to begin to speak
The rhythm makes us feel closer
To the freedom that we seek

Soon the preacher will stand
Ready to deliver a word
While the congregation holds on
To the message in song, we just heard

It gives us strength
It gives us power
Through our darkest days
Until that final hour

Limited by Race

When I accepted the job
I simply did not know
My race and often my gender
Would determine how far I could go

Racial exclusions and limitations
Was not listed in the description
But it didn't take me long
To realize that was the prescription

The paleness of your identity
Was an ascension to leadership roles
While darker classifications of color
Was a barrier to meeting goals

The higher you're ranked in title
The more money you're able to make
You can build wealth for your family
While charity is left for others to take

Retirement checks and benefits
Are calculated at a lower pay
Unmatched by years of service
Or the number of hours worked in a day

There are supervisors who will tell you
Just be glad you got the position
Though, I can assure you
That's not stated in the company's mission

NOTES:

NOTES:

NOTES:

For everyone joined together across demographics to build equity, unite in calls for humanity, and taking the time to read, reflect, and purchase this book...

THANK YOU!

Made in the USA
Columbia, SC
28 October 2023